Sweet Potato

(A Grumpy the Iguana and Green Parrot Adventure)

By: Susan Marie Chapman
Illustrated by: Natalia Loseva

For my daughter, Avery.
You are my sunshine.

Published 2022

Printed in the United States of America
Print ISBN: 978--------

Canoe Tree Press
4697 Main Street
Manchester, VT 05255
www.CanoeTreePress.com

Sweet Potato watched as
her brothers munched on squirmy bugs.

"Yuck," thought Sweet Potato. "No crawly critters for me!"

"We are owls," Daddy Screech Owl explained.
"Meat is what we eat."

"Well, I only like sweet potatoes and mangoes," she cried.

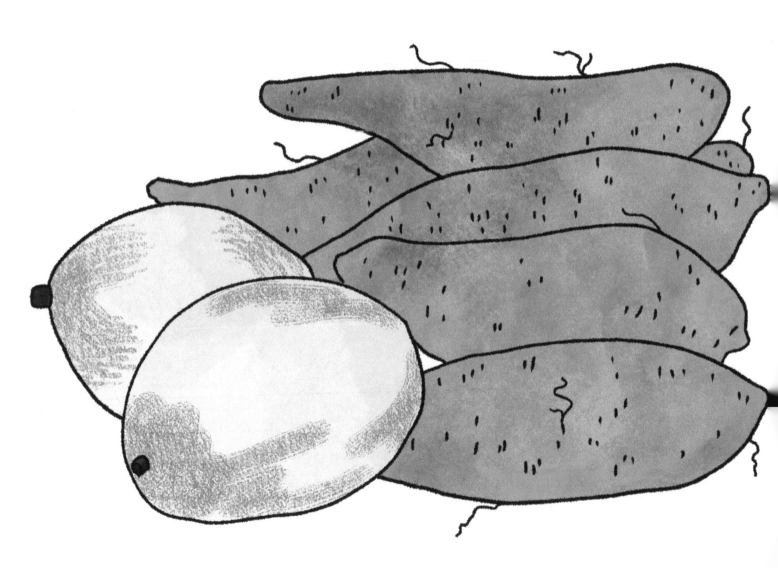

Mr. Screech Owl regretted ever feeding sweet potato fries to his three starving children.

He had discovered the fries in a trash can in the park. The boys refused to eat them, but the little girl cried for more.

This is how Sweet Potato got her name, which fit perfectly since her feathers were a burnt-orange color, just like a sweet potato.

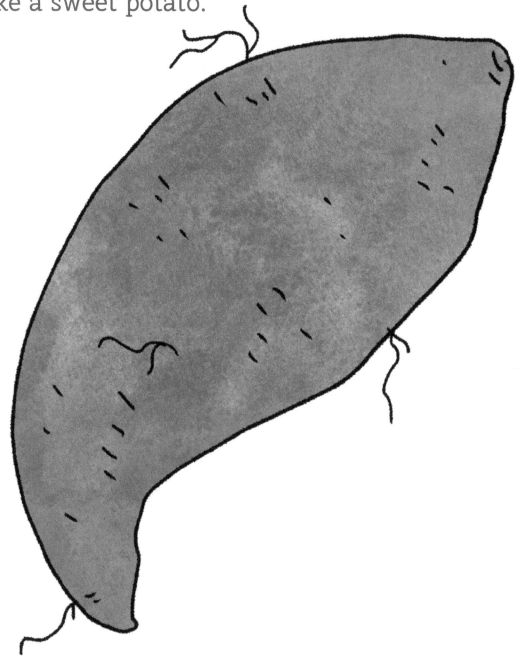

The Owl family had just finished their breakfast and were now sleepy; everyone except for Sweet Potato, that is.

"Mom, can I go and spend the day with Uncle Grumpy?" Sweet Potato pleaded.
"We usually sleep during the day and play at night, remember dear?" Mama Owl explained.

As soon as her family fell asleep, Sweet Potato quietly hopped out of the nest and made her way to Grumpy's house.

Grumpy was preparing a few snacks and a coconut filled with water. He was going to spend the day in the park.

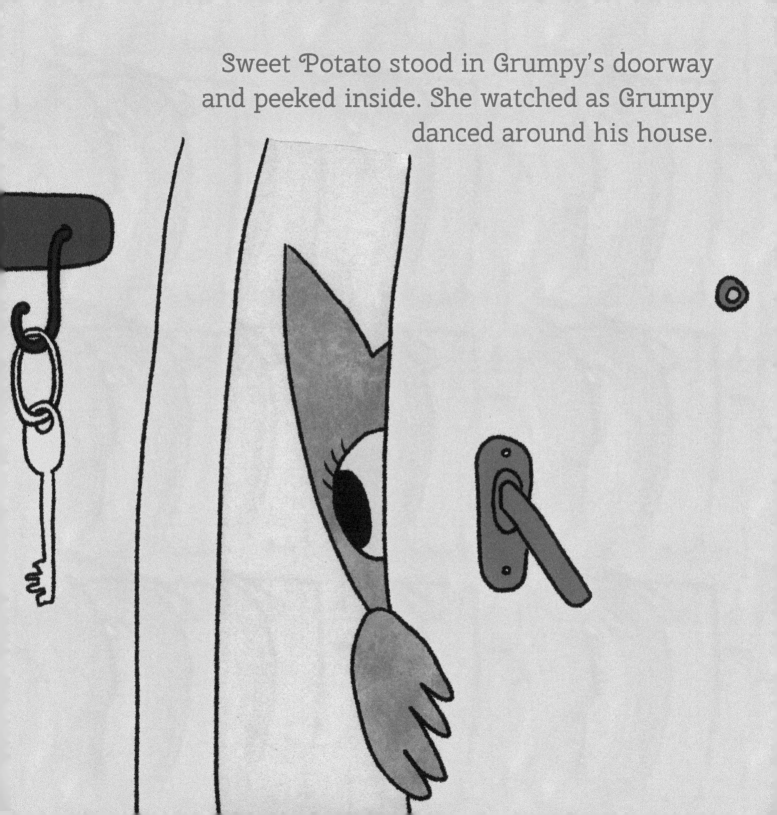

Sweet Potato stood in Grumpy's doorway and peeked inside. She watched as Grumpy danced around his house.

Sweet Potato started to giggle. Grumpy stopped dancing and turned around. "Who's there?" Grumpy inquired.
"It's me, Sweet Potato," she said as she hopped into the room.

"Aren't you supposed to be sleeping?" Grumpy asked.
"Well, no, I'm not tired," Sweet Potato answered.

Grumpy had a soft spot for this little baby owl. You see, Grumpy was there when Sweet Potato hatched and broke free from her egg. Mom and Dad hugged one another. Grumpy just cried. He had never witnessed a birth before. Sweet Potato was so tiny and wobbly and when she spotted Grumpy, she snuggled up against his face. Grumpy's heart just melted.

Grumpy now smiled at his little Screech Owl girl.
"Come on then, hop on," he said. Sweet Potato jumped up
and down and flapped her wings.
"Let's go, Uncle Grumpy!" she shouted with glee.

They made their way through the park until they reached Grumpy's favorite rock. "Here we are!" said Grumpy.

"I want to get some sun too!" Sweet Potato hooted, as she picked out a spot next to Grumpy.
"Maybe now you will get some sleep like you're supposed to, young lady," Grumpy said as he closed his eyes.

"When I grow up, I want to be an iguana just like you, Uncle Grumpy. Did you know that I do not eat bugs?" Sweet Potato continued.

"Well, I do love your company, but you should be asleep in the nest with your brothers right now," Grumpy answered. "Like your parents suggested."

"Remember, I was there when your mom and dad found each other in Flamingo Park. They were so in love," Grumpy recalled.
"I never get tired of hearing that story,"
Sweet Potato said, looking over at Grumpy.

Her brothers were boring. They had contests to see who could eat the most bugs. They would take turns throwing live bugs in the air, open their mouths to catch the bugs as they fell, and then bump shoulders.
Sweet Potato watched in utter disgust.

"I never want to play any bug games," she thought to herself. Sweet Potato was a rebel and had big plans for her future.

Sweet Potato slowly closed
her eyes. She was sleepy.
Grumpy started to doze off too.
His eyes were closed, but he
could still hear Sweet Potato
chatting away. "Boy, that girl
can talk," Grumpy laughed
to himself.

Just then, Grumpy heard a loud shrill cry. He jumped up. It was Mrs. Screech Owl and she looked upset.
"Sweet Potato!" Mrs. Owl cried. "I have been looking everywhere for you."

"Why aren't you in your nest asleep?" Mama Owl said sternly. "I was helping Grumpy get to his rock and then I was planning on coming straight home," Sweet Potato replied innocently.

"I was so worried about you," Mama Owl said as she hugged her little girl. "Owls are supposed to sleep all day and play all night."

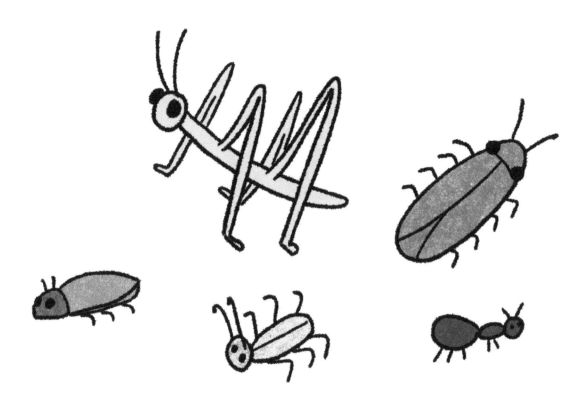

"Well, I'm different, right, Uncle Grumpy?" Sweet Potato said.

Grumpy put his hands out, and Sweet Potato placed her tiny wings on top.

"You must always listen to your parents, Sweet Potato. They are here to guide you from danger and teach you all the life skills that will help you become a beautiful young lady one day."

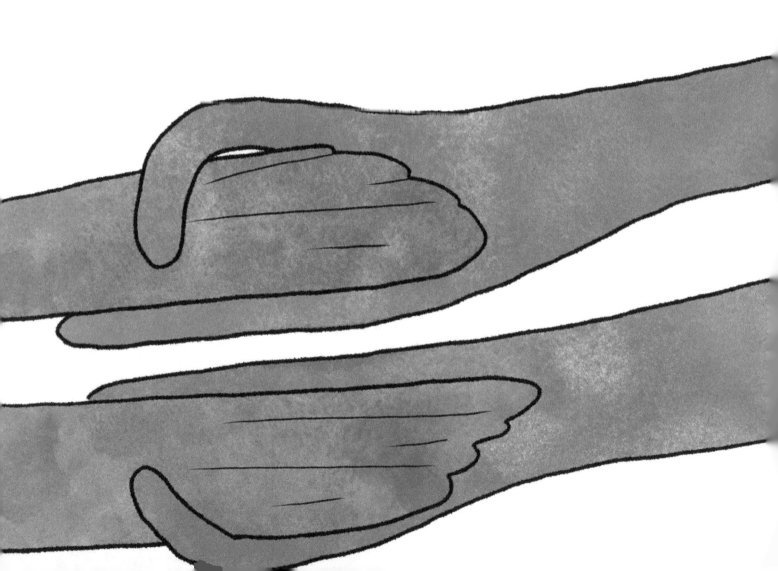

"Remember that your parents have your best interests at heart and they love you more than anything in the world," Grumpy concluded.

"Okay," said Sweet Potato as she grabbed onto her mom's wing. "I guess you are right, Uncle Grumpy. But, I'm still never going to eat bugs," she said as she yawned.

Grumpy laughed as he waved goodbye to mom and baby.
"See you tomorrow," he said. Mrs. Owl turned her head to give
Grumpy a stern look. "I meant tomorrow night,"
Grumpy corrected himself as he winked at Sweet Potato.
Sweet Potato just giggled.

THE END

CPSIA information can be obtained
at www.ICGtesting.com
Printed in the USA
BVHW021531300722
643392BV00002B/18